# BRIDPORT AND WEST BAY

## The buildings of the flax and hemp industry

Published by English Heritage, Kemble Drive, Swindon SN2 2GZ
www.english-heritage.org.uk
English Heritage is the Government's statutory adviser on all aspects of the historic environment.

© English Heritage 2006

Printing 10 9 8 7 6 5 4 3 2 1

Images (except as otherwise shown) © English Heritage, © English Heritage. NMR
or © Crown copyright. NMR.

First published 2006

ISBN-10  1 873 592 86 8
ISBN-13  978 1 873 592 86 1

Product code 51167

*British Library Cataloguing in Publication Data*
A CIP catalogue record for this book is available from the British Library.

Application for the reproduction of images should be made to the National Monuments Record. Every
effort has been made to trace the copyright holders and we apologise in advance for any unintentional
omissions, which we would be pleased to correct in any subsequent edition of this book.

The National Monuments Record is the public archive of English Heritage. For more information,
contact NMR Enquiry and Research Services, National Monuments Record Centre, Kemble Drive,
Swindon SN2 2GZ; telephone (01793) 414600.

Brought to publication by Rachel Howard, Publishing, English Heritage.
Page layout by George Hammond.
Printed in Belgium by Snoeck Ducaju.

Front cover
*Many of the varied houses along
South Street, Bridport, were
occupied by the families of rope,
twine and net makers for
centuries before the first factories
were built. [DP022155]*

Inside front cover
*Detail of Good's Yard warehouse.
[AA049594]*

# BRIDPORT AND WEST BAY

The buildings of the flax and hemp industry

Mike Williams

ENGLISH HERITAGE

# Contents

Frontispiece *The Hyde at Walditch was the Victorian residence of the Gundry family, owners of Court Mills and one of Bridport's most successful firms. An unusually wide variety of historic houses are associated with Bridport's flax and hemp industry.* [DP004837]

# Acknowledgements

This book is based on fieldwork and research by Mike Williams, Sheila Ely, Barry Jones and Alan Stoyel. Additional local research was carried out by Richard Sims. The photographs were taken by Mike Hesketh-Roberts and the maps and drawings prepared by Tony Berry, both of English Heritage. Many other people have also made valuable contributions to the project. The project team would like to thank John Cattell, Keith Falconer, Jill Guthrie, Nick Molyneux, Ian Savage, David Stuart and Andrew Vines of English Heritage, and Jo Witherden and Shelley Saltman of West Dorset District Council. Mike Bone provided advice on industrial archaeology. In Bridport, the staff of the Museum and the Coach House Local Studies Centre have been most helpful throughout the project. A wide range of archive material on the flax and hemp industry was made available by Frances Sanctuary and Jacquie Summers of the Museum of Net Manufacture, Uploders. Further research and advice was given by members of the Bridport History Society and the Somerset and Dorset Family History Society. In particular, the authors would like to thank the owners and occupiers of the buildings selected for study for kindly providing access for research.

*Bridport's industrial traditions depicted in sculpture, Bucky Doo Square, central [Bridport. DP000784]*

# Foreword

Bridport is the home of an ancient industry, the manufacture of goods from flax and hemp. Its story has long been known by historians, but the significance of its industrial buildings and landscapes has only recently come to light. The flax and hemp industry was established here by the beginning of the 13th century, a remarkably early date, when it was already of sufficiently high repute to be called upon to supply ropes and sailcloth for the king's navy. It survived many changes of fortune, and by the late 18th century Bridport flourished as the pre-eminent source of rope, twine and netting in South-West England. In its modern form the industry is still an important employer, having outlived most of the historic industries in other regions. In a country which is known throughout the world for its industrial heritage, Bridport's netting and cordage trade can proudly claim to represent one of the longest-surviving traditions of manufacturing industry.

The prolonged influence of the flax and hemp industry can be seen in the exceptional diversity of Bridport's industrial landscape, including the wide range of well-preserved historic housing, the distinctive walks used for spinning twine and rope and the buildings around the harbour at West Bay. Economic changes in the 20th century have left another legacy, however, with problems such as the empty buildings and run-down areas that are familiar to many industrial towns. This book aims to encourage a fresh understanding and appreciation of all the built remains of Bridport's industrial heritage, including those which have seen better days. The local townscapes of the flax and hemp industry are of great historic significance. It is hoped that they can be well treated as cornerstones of Bridport's heritage, and utilised as building blocks for the regeneration of its historic industrial areas.

Sir Neil Cossons OBE
Chairman of English Heritage

CHAPTER 1

# Bridport and the flax and hemp industry

The chief work of children is turning wheels for twine spinners, and most so employed are children, boys or girls as it happens. Twine spinners work in open spinning "walks" or "ways", planted with trees to keep off the sun, the turners sitting in a shed at the end, open on the side towards the walk, turning a small wheel by hand to twist the fibre for the spinner. Bridport is full of such "spinning ways", running from the backs of the houses like gardens, several side-by-side, with no separation. The number, however, is said to have greatly decreased of late years, it is estimated by one witness to a third of the former amount, owing to the great increase of the work done in the factories.

From the report of Mr J E White on the employment of children in Bridport's rope and twine manufacture, 1866[1].

Bridport has been an important centre for the production of rope, twine, netting and sailcloth, originally from flax and hemp, from the 13th century, and possibly earlier. The Bridport textile industry is one of the oldest documented industries in England, having survived in its original location long after most other early industries had moved to new areas. For eight centuries Bridport's industrial community has earned the town an international reputation for the quality of its products. By the 18th century the industry employed a high proportion of the local population, often providing work for men, women and children from the same family (Fig 1). Remarkably, some of the oldest industrial sites are still used for the manufacture of netting products today. Visitors are presented with the unusual combination of market town architecture with a wide variety of industrial buildings, some now disused, giving parts of Bridport an urban character which is unexpected in the Dorset countryside.

Figure 1 *Making up herring nets in Court Mills, late 19th century. The twine, net and sailcloth industries were the main source of work in Bridport for centuries, often employing several members of the same family. [Museum of Net Manufacture]*

1. Parliamentary Papers 1865–7 (36783) XXIV, 102 (5th report of the Children's Employment Commission), Report upon the Rope and Twine Manufacture by Mr J E White, 1866

This book describes the buildings and landscapes of Bridport's textile industry, and makes comparisons with those of historic textile industries in other parts of England. It concludes that the surviving sites should now be appreciated as a rare and important heritage resource, and that experience in other towns has demonstrated that the heritage of post-industrial areas can play a strong and viable role in the town's regeneration.

Local interest and enthusiasm for Bridport's history has led to the publication of a wide range of books, articles and exhibitions, some dealing specifically with aspects of the town's textile industry, but relatively little has been written specifically on its industrial buildings and landscapes. Buildings and open spaces provide a rich source of additional information about the history and working life of a town, and also largely define its visual character. The regional and national significance of Bridport's built environment has come to light following studies of its industrial archaeology, recent publications on the historic textile industries in other parts of England and an ongoing survey by English Heritage of textile industries in the South West. In comparison with these other areas, Bridport's industrial heritage is exceptionally early, highly distinctive and relatively well preserved.

Evidence of Bridport's industrial past can be readily seen by walking along the main streets, where a range of well-preserved houses and other building types offer clues to the town's history. Parts of South Street and East Street, for example, are fronted by the varied cottages of a community that was involved in industry for many generations. Consequently, these cottages are far more diverse in appearance and date than the terraced housing of other industrial towns (Fig 2). Closer to the town centre, the commercial and institutional buildings that are so typical of a country market town stand alongside the grand townhouses of a former prosperous class of merchants and industrialists. More evidence can be seen by exploring further, down the many alleys and back streets. Behind the cottages are parallel rows of unusually long and narrow gardens, some of which have been built-over with immensely long sheds and other industrial structures, now mostly disused. These are the remains of the spinning walks that were used for making twine and rope.

Figure 2 *Many of the cottages fronting Bridport's main streets were occupied by twine spinners or net makers employed as outworkers by the larger factories. Bridport's industrial housing contrasts with that of factory towns in its variety of building materials, architectural features and wide date range.* [DP000748]

Figure 3 *Gundry Lane, viewed from South Street, shows the contrast between market town buildings and industrial architecture that characterises much of Bridport's townscape. [DP000766]*

Other parts of the town centre are even more industrial in character, with large 19th-century warehouses and textile mills which at first seem out of place in a rural area (Fig 3).

A mile south of the town is Bridport Harbour, later renamed West Bay, which was crucial to the economy of the town and, significantly, also retains a high proportion of its historic buildings. It was built with extensive warehousing and shipbuilding facilities, and stands on the only site suitable for the construction of an industrial harbour along an exposed stretch of coastline. The development of the harbour in the mid-18th century fuelled a resurgence of the Bridport textile industry and triggered a dramatic expansion of the town. By the early 19th century the larger textile firms occupied warehouses at the harbour and had ships built in the adjacent shipyard, supporting a worldwide trade in goods and raw materials.

The main reason that the flax and hemp industry became established in West Dorset was probably the suitability of the fertile, well-drained soils and relatively mild climate for the growing of the raw fibre (Fig 4). The industry had workers based in villages and farms throughout the countryside surrounding Bridport, complementing its other role as a market town serving an agricultural region. The town's trade also benefited from its location on a traditional east–west route along the

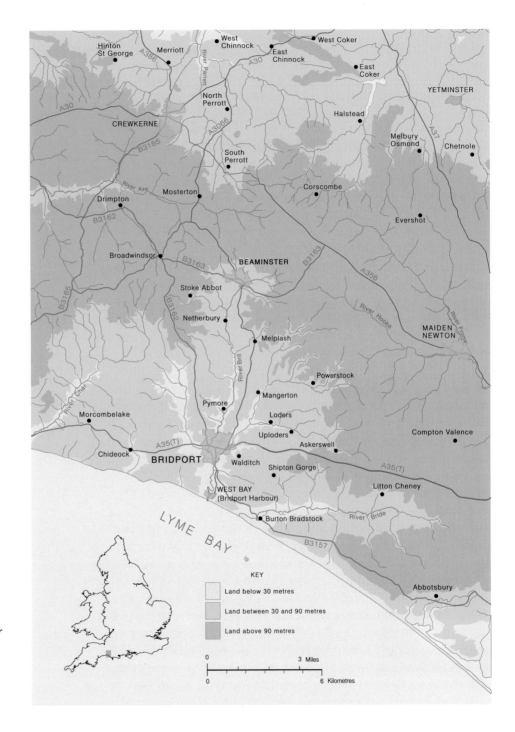

Figure 4 *The hilly topography and fertile, well-drained soils of West Dorset and South Somerset were well suited for flax and hemp growing. The influence of the industry was felt over a large area of the surrounding countryside. Nearby villages and towns eventually specialised in the production of particular types of netting or cloth.*

5

south coast. By the 18th century, flax and hemp seed was imported by textile merchants for distribution to local growers, and country mills were built or adapted to process the harvested crops. As the industry expanded in the 19th century, locally-grown fibres were eventually replaced by a wider range of imported raw materials. Various estimates have been published of the size of the hinterland which was directly influenced by the Bridport textile industry, most describing areas with a radius of up to twenty miles. However, in comparison with other well-known historic industrial textile towns a remarkably high proportion of Bridport's population were employed in the textile industry. Estimates of the size of the workforce suggest that the numbers employed would have varied considerably with the economic demand for hemp and flax products. For example, in the late 18th century about 1,800 people (out of a population of 3,100) are said to have worked in the industry in Bridport itself, with a further 7,000 in the surrounding area.

The early origin of Bridport's textile industry is of great historic interest, but little has been published comparing Bridport with other industrial areas. In the medieval period there were several other well-known centres of the textile industry, and in later periods important flax and hemp industries also developed in other regions of England, Scotland and Northern Ireland. Rope making was particularly widespread, especially in areas with shipbuilding industries. What distinguishes Bridport from all these places, however, is the long-term success of its textile industry. Many of the other medieval textile industries declined when the focus of manufacturing shifted to water-powered mills, and later still to large urban conurbations. In Bridport, factories did not quickly replace the old methods as had happened in other areas, but were combined with the revival of a traditional industry that already had a skilled workforce. The long development of Bridport's industry with its skilled and flexible workforce enabled Briport to be competitive in the new factory-based economy. By the beginning of the 20th century the largest Bridport firms were managing twine and net factories in other parts of England and Scotland, and by the middle of the century they were managing factories in other countries around the world. The unrivalled continuity of the flax and hemp industry not only shaped the appearance of Bridport and became rooted in its traditions, but was also synonymous with the name of the town itself. When decades of mergers and takeovers had left just one very large net-making firm in the 1960s it adopted the title Bridport-Gundry, derived from the names of the earlier firms of Bridport Industries and Joseph Gundry, linking the identity of the town with its historic staple trade.

## A brief history of Bridport and its textile industry

The earliest documentary evidence of the industry, referenced in numerous publications, is a record of payment for a large quantity of sails and cordage in 1211, which was followed by an order from King John for Bridport rope and cloth to supply the navy in 1213. The large size and prestigious nature of this order suggests that a well-known rope and sailcloth industry was already established in the area before the early 13th century.

The town certainly had earlier origins. Its ancient core was probably an Anglo-Saxon burh in the area of South Street and St Mary's Church, although it is unlikely that any above-ground structures survive from this period. This was a strategic, defendable site, located on the traditional route along the coast and bounded by rivers to the west, east and south. Medieval expansion took place to the north, with the creation of new east–west roads into the town and the extension of the settled area along West Street, East Street and the north end of South Street. The extent of medieval development is suggested by the regular pattern of long boundary walls at right angles to the streets, which indicate the probable outlines of former burgage plots (Fig 5). These medieval plots, which took the form of parallel narrow strips extending behind the houses fronting the main streets, can still be detected in many historic towns and are recognised as one of the defining features of medieval townscapes. They were used for cultivation or small-scale industry, many of those in Bridport being used for making twine or rope. The evidence of medieval property boundaries, streets and alleys is particularly well preserved in

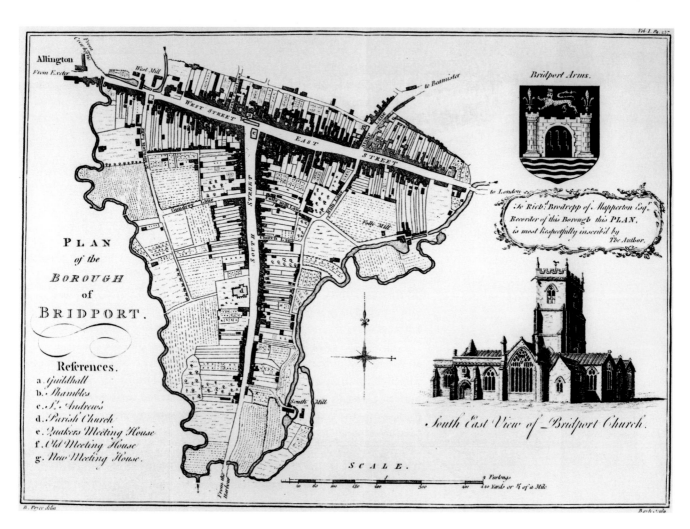

Figure 5 *The street plan of central Bridport has changed surprisingly little.
This 1774 map clearly shows the remains of the medieval burgage plots, some of
which were used as spinning walks, together with several mills used for textiles.
[From Hutchins, J 1774* The History and Antiquities of the County of
Dorset....*Vol 1, 233. London: Bowyer and Nichols]*

Bridport, partly as a result of the influence of the textile industry, and forms an important feature of the present-day townscape.

In the later medieval period the Bridport rope industry received legal protection from external competition, and by the 16th century the town was a nationally-important centre for the production of rope for the navy. In the 17th century some of the notable family businesses which eventually dominated the Bridport textile industry were established as flax and hemp merchants. Several of the larger industrial sites were probably first occupied in this period, although the extant buildings were added later. However, in spite of all this early industrial activity, Bridport does not appear to have grown significantly between the 16th and the mid-18th century. The population was badly affected by plagues in the 16th and 17th centuries, and the industry later suffered because of the transfer of much of the production to the naval dockyards and increasing competition from other regions.

The most successful period for the flax and hemp trade was a dramatic revival from the late 18th to the late 19th century. The relative prosperity of this period saw the construction of houses for the merchant classes and the rebuilding of many of the outworkers' cottages. Improvements to the main streets and some public buildings, including the building of the Town Hall, were initiated by the Bridport Improvement Act of 1785. The organisation of the industry and the appearance of its buildings changed significantly but, in contrast with many other industrial areas of England, the new factories did not completely replace the older methods of production and operated alongside the walks and workshops. In Bridport the smaller textile businesses thrived as the industry expanded, most relying on work which was put out by the merchants and factory owners. Between the mid-19th and the mid-20th century, mergers and takeovers led to a reduction in the number of smaller firms, while production moved from the independent walks and workshops to the factory sites.

The expansion of the flax and hemp industry was closely linked to the growth of international trade that followed the development of Bridport Harbour. The harbour was rebuilt in the mid-18th century to exploit a prosperous trade with Newfoundland, which also benefited

Figure 6 *Francis Newbery's impression of Bridport Harbour in the late 19th century. The harbour was essential to the later growth of the textile industry and included a successful shipbuilding yard from the late 18th century.*
*[Part of a series of murals in Bridport Town Hall by Newbery, 1924]*

Figure 7 *Bridport Harbour was still used by commercial shipping in the 1890s, although its relevance to the flax and hemp trade was by then in decline. [Bridport Museum, W32]*

other ports in Dorset and Devon. It enabled Bridport's merchants to develop a specialised trade in flax and hemp products. Nets and cordage were exported for use in the Newfoundland fisheries and salted fish brought back on the return trip. By the mid-19th century a thriving community had grown around the harbour, including a 13-acre shipyard, new streets, numerous warehouses, and a variety of housing for workers and merchants (Fig 6). International trade remained important to Bridport's flax and hemp industry, although the proportion of that trade handled by the harbour declined after the introduction of the railways in the 1850s (Fig 7).

## Labour, processes and products in the flax and hemp industry

The flax and hemp industry employed people in an extremely wide range of occupations in the Bridport area, ranging from agricultural labour to working in factories and warehouses, outworking in cottages, workshops and walks and even the building and crewing of merchant vessels based at the harbour. The employers and the workforce came from all levels of Bridport society, with men, women and children each concentrating on particular types of work, often in conditions which would today be considered extremely unhealthy. Flax was most commonly used for weaving cloth, such as linen, sailcloth and canvas, and for spinning into the more supple twines used in netting. Hemp was a coarser fibre which was mainly used for making stronger rope and twine, such as fishing line and the wide variety of rope used on ships. By the late 19th century other types of raw fibre were imported for use in cordage and netting, including cotton, sisal and jute.

The diverse nature of the work reflected the many different processes involved in converting flax and hemp crops into textile products. Both plants had to be prepared before they could be used for spinning, and much of the preparation was carried out in farms and mills around the town (Fig 8). The hard, woody stems were initially softened by retting, either by soaking them in open tanks of water or by simply leaving them to rot in the open fields. The latter process, known as dew retting, was the traditional method in Dorset, although tank retting was used in a temporary revival of the industry in the mid-20th century (Fig 9). Flax was then dried and swingled, a powered process by which the woody parts were discarded from the useful fibre. Hemp was a much taller plant with a thicker stem from which the fibre was obtained by a process involving hammering with heavier machinery in a balling mill. The bundles of fibre were made ready for spinning by heckling, or combing, in which they were aligned by drawing them through rows of metal spikes (Fig 10). This was very physical work carried out by men, and was usually located in a separate building because it created a dusty atmosphere. The shorter fibres obtained as a by-product of heckling, known as tow, were separated and used for the production of lower-grade yarns.

Figure 8 *Locally-grown cut flax being stooked for drying in the mid-20th century. [Museum of Net Manufacture]*

Figure 9 *Retting flax at Netherbury, north of Bridport, mid-20th century. [Museum of Net Manufacture]*

Figure 10 *Drawing hemp by hand in a Bridport Mill. [Museum of Net Manufacture]*

Figure 11 *Work in a traditional Bridport twine walk. The spinners on the right are pulling out yarn from raw fibre wrapped around their waists, while twist is applied by the assistant cranking the jack in the turn house on the left. The yarn is supported on skirders attached to trees. [Part of a series of murals in Bridport Town Hall by Newbery, 1924]*

For centuries, the spinning of yarn, twine and rope was done by hand in open walks, often by women and young children. An open walk was typically a long, narrow, segregated area, sometimes a former burgage plot, extending behind a house or mill or alongside a field boundary. To make yarn, a bundle of prepared fibre was drawn out by hand by an operative moving slowly, backwards, along the walk. The women who performed this part of the process were referred to as spinners. The twist was applied by an assistant, usually a child, who turned a machine known as a jack located at the end of the walk (Fig 11). Twine was also produced in walks, in a process that involved twisting together several lengths of yarn; rope was made by twisting together, or laying, several lengths of twine. Various finishing processes might be applied after spinning, such as the tarring of rope for use at sea and the sizing and polishing of twine for use in netting.

Powered machinery was in use in the flax and hemp industry in the South West by the mid-18th century, although it was already in use in other regions. By the late 19th century the covered walks and steam-powered mills of Bridport had adopted a range of different types of machinery, some of which was powered, to improve the production of twine and rope. The factory workforce comprised both men and women. Unusually, the use of traditional methods, including open walks, continued in Bridport long after powered machinery in factories dominated the textile industries of other regions. One reason for this was probably that the hand-operated processes in the walks were more flexible than the early types of machinery, and could be readily adapted to make a wider variety of twines and ropes.

The weaving of cloth and the braiding of nets also continued as hand processes for an unusually long period in Bridport. The work was put out to home-based workers, usually women, both in the town and the surrounding area. Some villages specialised in sailcloth or particular types of netting. In other parts of the country handloom weaving was concentrated in loomshops before the introduction of powerlooms, and it is likely that some of the workshop buildings in the Bridport area were also used for weaving. The first powerlooms were introduced in 1851, but by then Bridport had begun to specialise more in the production of

netting. Net-making machines had been introduced by the 1860s and were followed by a succession of improved types of machinery at the larger factories (Fig 12), although some types of netting continued to be hand-braided throughout the 20th century (Fig 13).

Figure 12 *(above, left) Net-making machinery in a Bridport mill, early 20th century. [Museum of Net Manufacture]*

Figure 13 *(above, right) The hand-braiding of billiard table pockets in an East Street cottage, early 1970s. [By permission of J E Manners]*

## The recent history of the Bridport netting industry

The manufacture of netting products is still one of Bridport's best-known industries and an important source of employment, although the workforce is much reduced compared to that of the industry's heyday and most of the netting itself is now made abroad from man-made fibre. Many of the old factory sites have remained in use, which has helped preserve much of Bridport's industrial heritage. In the 20th century the local industry survived by consolidating the number of firms and diversifying into new markets, while those in many other textile-producing areas of England did not. Demand for traditional products, such as rope for sailing ships, was replaced by demand for a wide range of new goods including made-up nets for commercial fishing, market gardening and sports goods

Figure 14 *(above, left) Labels from a variety of products, including fishing nets, sports nets and fishing twine, made by firms in the Bridport Industries group, mid-20th century. [Museum of Net Manufacture]*

Figure 15 *(above, right) Fishing net production at Court Mills, c1930. [Museum of Net Manufacture]*

(Fig 14). The construction of drift and trawl nets was important to Bridport for many decades, each one requiring hundreds of yards of netting with floats, beams and other attachments (Fig 15). Government orders for military products dominated the industry during both World Wars, including camouflage nets, pull-throughs for cleaning rifles and even anti-submarine nets. Bridport firms have manufactured sports nets from the late 19th century and locally-made products can still be seen at many high-profile events; Edwards Sports, now based at North Mills, were the sole manufacturer of the original patented football net. The largest firm today is AmSafe Bridport, which occupies the former Bridport-Gundry site at Court Mills and operates other manufacturing sites in the USA and Sri Lanka. The firm manufactures high-tech aircraft cargo-restraint nets and military products for global markets. At the opposite end of the range of netting businesses, another significant development for the town in recent years has been the re-emergence of a number of small firms occupying redundant industrial buildings. Utilising skills which are familiar to workers in the Bridport area, smaller businesses have the flexibility to meet the demand which still exists for a wide variety of netting products while maintaining the community's broad involvement with its traditional industry.

CHAPTER 2

# Buildings and landscapes of the Bridport flax and hemp industry

The enduring history of flax and hemp manufacture is strongly reflected in the physical character not only of Bridport itself, but also the villages in the surrounding countryside and the harbour at West Bay. The influence of the trade and its entrepreneurs was widely felt and affected many aspects of the built environment. In addition to the walks and mills themselves, evidence of the industry can be seen in the form of the warehouses, workshops and factory buildings; in the distinctive types of housing built for the outworkers, factory workers and merchants; in the shipping warehouses and settlement at the harbour; and even in the shape of the gardens and property boundaries.

The revival of the industry from the late 18th century saw the continued use of many of the spinning walks and workshops in the older parts of the town, while new types of industrial buildings appeared on the outskirts. These new industrial suburbs dramatically increased the size of Bridport and were characterised by two quite different types of architecture. In the first, complexes of large textile mills and related factory buildings appeared which were comparable to those in other regions but with features specific to the needs of the local textile industry. In the second, extensive areas of new spinning walks, workshops and housing were built in a layout similar to those in the town centre, creating new groups of highly distinctive linear buildings. This unusual mix of building types characterised Bridport's industrial landscape, where outworkers and small firms continued to use the old methods alongside the new factories with their powered machinery.

## Spinning walks

The earliest visible evidence of Bridport's textile industry is not found in the surviving buildings but in the outline of the gardens and other open spaces in the older parts of the town, where many of the spinning walks were established in former burgage plots (Fig 16). The later expansion of the Bridport textile industry saw the increased use of these open walks, in a period when the remains of medieval townscapes elsewhere were often

*Central Bridport, 1999. The T-shaped pattern of medieval market streets is probably Bridport's earliest historic feature. [SY 4692/76 18369/02]*

under threat from redevelopment. The use of some of the walks for spinning in Bridport continued throughout the 19th century, long after factory methods dominated the textile industries of other regions. Many of the open walks were gradually converted into covered walks by the addition of new buildings, but their continued use for spinning meant that the scale and proportions of the original plot were retained (Fig 17). A significant number of the former open walks are still enclosed by 18th- or 19th-century boundary walls, usually built in brick.

From the mid-18th to the mid-19th centuries areas of new open walks were set out on the outskirts of Bridport. Good examples from this period can still be seen to the west of St Michael's Lane and in parts of North and West Allington. The new walks were laid out in the same proportions as the ancient walks (ie very long and narrow) indicating that the older plots still provided efficient sites for spinning. This retention of the old methods in Bridport was unusual at a time when elsewhere in the

*Figure 16 Many of the long gardens in Bridport, such as these to the south of East Street, originated as medieval burgage plots and were later used as open spinning walks. [AA030997]*

*Figure 17 The distinctive pattern of narrow open and covered walks is clearly evident on both sides of East Street. [NMR 18369/04 SY 4692/78]*

country textile industries were being completely re-organised and re-engineered.

The townscape of the open walks included a range of other smaller industrial buildings, but today well-preserved examples of these smaller structures are rarer than the walks themselves (Fig 18). Some walks retain a turn house or twine store at one end. These were small buildings, often with an open-sided ground floor facing the walk, where the twine and an operative could be protected from the elements. In many cases the turn house had upper floors used for preparing the raw fibre and the storage of twine. Other ancillary buildings included a variety of workshops used for processes such as heckling, net making or the tarring of twine or rope. The yarns were supported and separated from one another by skirders, a type of wooden horizontal bracket placed at intervals along the walk. In Bridport the skirders were sometimes attached to the trunks of fruit trees grown in the walks (see Fig 11). Unfortunately, no surviving *in situ* skirders have been identified (but *see* Fig 22).

In the late 19th and early 20th century the open walks were increasingly replaced with extremely long and narrow gabled buildings, which are often referred to as covered walks. In addition to the conversion of the open walks, completely new covered walks were erected on greenfield sites, for example in West Allington and at North Mills (Fig 19). Built specifically for the spinning of twine or rope, these buildings are striking examples of the relationship between external form and internal function in industrial architecture (Fig 20). They were also built in other textile-producing areas, although few other towns, if any, had similar concentrations of walks to Bridport, and Bridport now retains more covered walks than any other former cordage-producing area in the South West. As specialised industrial buildings, most have little or no ornamental treatment but include a range of functional features. The larger one-and-a-half or two-storeyed covered walks retain good evidence that their ground-floor walls were originally open to provide ample ventilation, possibly for drying finished twine. A few of the walks retain shaft boxes and other features indicating that they were powered, although the use of partly hand-operated processes remained commonplace.

Figure 18 *Small industrial buildings were essential features of Bridport's walks, such as these to the south of East Street. Many were demolished when the walks fell out of use. [AA031001]*

Figure 19 *The largest surviving covered walk in Bridport is at North Mills. [AA031003]*

Figure 20 *A rare 19th-century photograph (hand tinted) showing the interior of a Bridport covered walk. [Museum of Net Manufacture]*

Figure 21 *Parts of East Street illustrate how industrial buildings and housing were gradually added to the open walks in the 19th century, retaining the form of the earlier plots. The former covered-walk buildings on the right have been re-used for the manufacture of netting products. [DP001483]*

## East Street: cottages and walks

Bridport's best-preserved group of open and part-covered walks in an area of former burgage plots is located on the south side of East Street. Other notable examples survive on the opposite side of the street and also on South Street. The present-day property boundaries along East Street are very similar to those shown on 18th- and 19th- century maps. Most of the extant cottages, industrial buildings and boundary walls have been altered or extended in many phases from the 18th century, but this rebuilding has enhanced rather than destroyed the traditional scale of the area.

Documentary evidence indicates that many cordage and netting makers were based here in the 19th century, and one row of buildings in a former twine walk is still used for the manufacture of netting products today (Fig 21). Most of the plots are now used as long narrow gardens or yards, but retain a variety of structures relating to their industrial past, including boundary walls, workshops, extensions to cottages and several possible examples of former turn houses at the ends of the walks. In the 19th century new housing was added in some of the plots behind the front cottages but often respected the existing property boundaries. The compact form of the new housing, such as in Seymour Place, ensured that the linear form of the plots was retained, and that the covered passages entering the plots from East Street remained in use.

## Textile mills and factories

The introduction of factory methods of production was central to the success of Bridport's flax and hemp trade from the early 19th century. The new textile mills influenced the economy of the whole town, employing large numbers of outworkers and creating a local demand for a wide range of industrial goods. A number of historically-significant early mills have been demolished, but the surviving sites cover an exceptionally wide range of dates and illustrate most of the main stages in the development of textile-mill architecture. They include examples of the mid-18th-century workshops that preceded the factory system, large multi-storeyed mills built for water power and steam power, north-light sheds built to contain netting machinery and good examples of the single-storeyed factory buildings which began to replace multi-storeyed mills in the early 20th century. Bridport's textile mills had architectural similarities with those in other areas, but the organisation of the new factory-based industry was significantly different. They continued to rely on outworking even after the introduction of powered machinery, especially for the production of items that were difficult to make with machines. In the 19th century Bridport firms produced an unusual variety of goods, avoiding the trend towards specialisation seen in other textile industries. Consequently, Bridport's factories included a varied collection of ancillary buildings, in addition to the mills themselves, with features specific to the manufacture of a wide range of flax or hemp products.

Figure 22 *The northern part of Court Mills, photographed from the roof of the original building around 1890. The yard includes part of an open walk, with* in situ *skirders. [Museum of Net Manufacture]*

## Court Mills

Court Mills is the largest textile-mill complex in Dorset and the oldest extant factory site in Bridport. It is historically associated with the firm of Bridport-Gundry, a late 20th-century amalgamation of the town's main surviving textile manufacturers. The firm originated in the mid-17th century and occupied part of the site under Joseph Gundry by the 1760s. Court Mills was a centre of cordage and netting production throughout the 19th and 20th centuries, developing into an extensive complex of steam-powered buildings and sheds, along with open and covered walks (Fig 22). During the 20th century Gundry's expanded, taking over smaller firms both in Bridport and in other regions. The business finally merged with Bridport Industries, who were based in the St Michael's Lane area, in 1963, after which it traded as Bridport-Gundry. More recent changes have seen the site managed as part of a global business by Bridport Aviation in the 1990s and by AmSafe Bridport, the current occupiers, from 2002. Specialised aircraft-cargo and military netting products are still manufactured at Court Mills, representing an exceptionally long period of continuous use for an English textile mill.

Figure 23 *The original building at Court Mills was probably built as a workshop or warehouse. [AA031007]*

   The oldest surviving building, located by the south entrance to the site, probably originated as a warehouse or workshop in the late 18th century but is now used as offices (Fig 23). Several extensions were

added later, two of which are dated 1838 and 1844. In this period the site was not water- or steam-powered, since the firm was primarily a putting-out business and used flax twine made at the nearby Pymore Mills. From the mid-19th century Court Mills was expanded in several more phases and extended over a large area to the north, which included some demolition and rebuilding. By the end of the century the complex was huge, but did not include any of the multi-storeyed mills that typified other textile-producing areas. The main buildings were extensive one- and two-storeyed sheds built for spinning, netmaking machines and the finishing of twine and nets. The complex included a central engine and boiler house and a two-storeyed engineering workshop, which is now Bridport's only example of late 19th-century fireproof construction.

Figure 24 *North Mills at its greatest extent, with water- and steam-powered mills, warehouses, housing and the largest covered walks in Bridport. [Museum of Net Manufacture]*

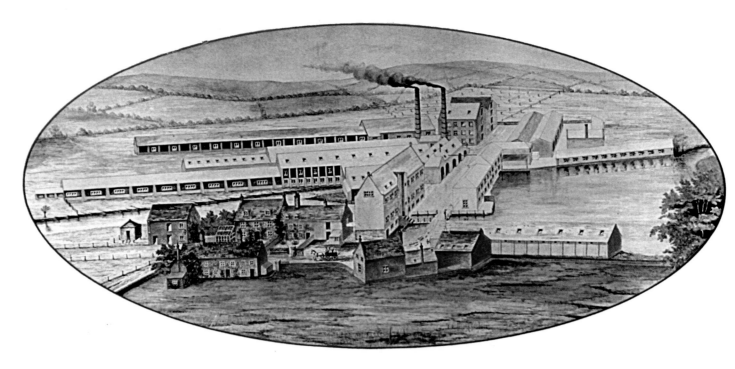

## North Mills

North Mills was established in the early 19th century as a large water- and steam-powered complex, just beyond the northern edge of the town and about half a mile upstream from Court Mills. It was used for the manufacture of twine, netting and sailcloth by William Hounsell and Company, another well-known Bridport firm which was founded in the 17th century. In the mid-to-late 19th century Hounsell's developed an extensive international trade in cordage and netting products. By that time North Mills had developed into a substantial site, including several powered mills, flax warehouses, north-light sheds and covered walks (Fig 24). In the mid-20th century the site was absorbed into the residential suburbs of Bridport and many of its earliest buildings were demolished, including the original water-powered mill with its adjoining pond. The largest extant building is a large, well-preserved three-storeyed warehouse, built in two phases during the mid-19th century. To the north of this, the complex comprises a series of late 19th- and 20th-century sheds with an attached engine house. The surviving part of the covered walks at North Mills now forms the largest walk building in Bridport (*see* Fig 19).

## Priory Mills

Priory Mills was built as a steam-powered flax-spinning mill in 1838. Today it retains the best-preserved mid-19th-century textile mill buildings in Bridport (Fig 25). It was later expanded with the addition of powered weaving and net-braiding machinery, creating a fully-integrated factory. In contrast with Court Mills, it has a number of similarities with textile mills in other regions, including its external proportions, power system and internal construction. It was occupied by Stephen Whetham and Sons, one of the most prominent 19th-century firms in Bridport. As an integrated factory, Priory Mills carried out all stages in the manufacture of twine, netting and sailcloth from raw flax and hemp. This firm was the first to introduce powerlooms to Bridport in 1851.

The stone-built principal buildings comprise a three-storeyed mill of eight bays and a parallel three-storeyed ancillary building of seven bays.

The mill was powered from an internal beam-engine house in the north-end bay, with steam supplied by an attached external boiler house. The floors are of heavy-timbered construction, with thick planks mounted directly on the beams, without using joists (Fig 26). This unusual type of construction was used to improve the strength and fire resistance of mill floors; the heavy beams and boards would char in a fire but not collapse. The smaller ancillary building is of similar date but has more conventional joisted floors. Steam-powered shafting was inserted later into its ground floor, but it may have originally been a workshop or warehouse. The two buildings are linked at the north end by a later north-light shed of three bays. A mid-19th-century house stands by the north boundary of the site, its position suggesting it was built to accommodate a site manager.

Figure 25 *Priory Mills, with part of the arched window of the internal engine house just visible on the right. [DP000775]*

Figure 26 *The unusually heavy timber ceilings of Priory Mills are a 19th-century design feature to improve strength and fire resistance. [AA046492]*

## Pymore Mills

Pymore was another large flax-mill complex, jointly owned by the Gundry's of Court Mills and other Bridport merchants, which included its own housing and other community buildings about a mile north of the town. It originated in the late 18th century, although it has changed considerably in recent years and most of the earlier mill buildings have been demolished. Two well-preserved mid-19th-century flax warehouses still overlook the north end of the site, however, separated by late 19th-century, steam-powered sheds with an engine house (Figs 27 and 28).

Figure 27 *The large flax warehouses at Pymore Mills indicate the scale of the complex in the 19th century. Most of the mill buildings themselves have been demolished. [DP000796]*

Figure 28 *Pymore, c1940, when the mills, warehouses, walks and drying grounds were still in use. [Museum of Net Manufacture]*

The warehouses are of three-storeys and of similar proportions to others at the larger flax mills in Dorset and Somerset, with symmetrical front elevations and a central row of loading doors. Relatively large warehouses may have been needed because the Pymore Flax Mill Company was a supplier of flax twine to other local manufacturers in the Bridport area.

## Workshops and warehouses

In contrast with the scale of the mills, which appeared mainly on the edges of Bridport, a number of smaller industrial workshops combined with warehousing were built in the town-centre side streets and back lanes from the late 18th to the mid-19th century. These distinctive buildings are of similar size, proportions and materials to contemporary housing, but without original domestic features. Their windows and doors are typical of modest industrial buildings (Fig 29). Most are of two or three storeys and three bays in length, usually with central loading doors to each storey, facing the street. They provided adaptable well-lit floorspace on a scale that was suitable for smaller businesses. Some were built at the ends of open walks and were associated with rope or twine production, and others are known to have been used for net making, although these adaptable buildings were also suitable for use by other industries.

Figure 29 *A typical Bridport workshop on Folly Mill Lane, now converted into housing. [AA045004]*

Six well-preserved examples of Bridport's traditional industrial workshops have been identified and several others are known to have existed but have subsequently been demolished. They represent an unusual building type, smaller than the loomshops seen in other areas, such as Gloucestershire, and indicate the continued importance of small firms in Bridport after the introduction of factories. Some were purpose built, others contain evidence of early changes of use. No. 40 St Michael's Lane, for example, is a three-storeyed workshop/warehouse that originally adjoined three parallel open walks to the rear (Fig 30). The front elevation contains a series of blocked windows and doors, however,

suggesting that it may have been built as three smaller workshops or cottages, before being converted into one unit.

Larger purpose-built warehouses can be seen at the mill sites and in the town centre. They were needed for the supply of raw materials to outworkers and for the temporary storage of materials and products at factories (Fig 31). Bridport has several examples of warehouses associated with the residences of early industrialists and merchants. Some of the better-preserved 18th- and 19th-century town houses had loading doors in their front or side elevations and other non-domestic features which suggest that they formerly incorporated some sort of warehousing (Fig 32). The larger firms also occupied parts of the warehouses at the harbour.

## The warehouse of Stephen Whetham and Sons

This prominent three-storeyed stone building is one of the largest warehouses in Bridport and is a prominent feature of the town centre; the interior was destroyed by fire in the late 1990s, but the building has been restored and remains in use as a depository (Fig 33). It comprises two

Figure 30 *(above, left) This mid-18th-century warehouse at No. 40 St Michael's Lane, built at the end of three parallel walks, is one of the earliest buildings in the South-West Quadrant. [AA049072]*

Figure 31 *(above, right) Bales of Italian hemp outside the warehouse of North Mills, 1945. [Museum of Net Manufacture]*

Figure 32 *(opposite, left) A good example of the combination of domestic architecture with taking-in doors for warehousing, on Downes Street. [AA045006]*

Figure 33 *(opposite, right) The mid-19th-century warehouse of Stephen Whetham and Sons, Gundry Lane. [AA042472]*

mid-19th-century phases, with the original six bays at the south end and a further six bays added to the north. The addition was built in 1862 and is lit by small square windows in alternate bays, suggesting that it provided secure storage. The original external doors, including a row of loading doors, all opened into a walled yard entered from Gundry Lane via a gate with stone piers. The entrance was overseen by an office lit by a bay window. The warehouse was built close to the townhouse of Stephen Whetham, the proprietor of Priory Mills (*see* Fig 37), and together with the gardens and the restored Coach House on Gundry Lane, forms an important historic group.

## Housing

Houses are the most numerous and diverse type of historic building in Bridport. Their distinctive and well-preserved façades make a vital contribution to the town's architectural character. Many of Bridport's houses were occupied by industrial workers or supervisors and reflect different aspects of the town's long association with the flax and hemp industry. Others were associated with the wide range of non-industrial occupations that were also found in a market town. Housing associated with the Bridport flax and hemp industry can be grouped into three main types: the cottages occupied by outworkers; the more regular 19th-century terraces which were usually occupied by factory workers; and a variety of larger houses occupied by the factory managers, merchants and industrialists.

### Outworkers' cottages

A wide variety of outworkers' cottages can be seen in East Street, South Street, North Allington and the South-West Quadrant (Figs 34 and 35). Many were occupied by twine spinners and net makers who worked at home, although other occupiers were involved with more typical market-town trades. Most are probably on the site of earlier houses and show evidence of rebuilding in the 18th and 19th century, when the flax

Figure 34 *(left) The rows of cottages fronting South Street illustrate some of the wide range of 18th- and 19th-century house types in Bridport, many of which were occupied by textile outworkers. This variety of industrial housing contrasts with the uniform terraces found in many other industrial towns. [DP005884, DP005891 and DP005889]*

Figure 35 *(right) Early 19th-century outworkers' cottages were amongst the first buildings in the South-West Quadrant, the industrial suburb to the west of St Michael's Lane (see page 40). [AA042470]*

and hemp industry prospered. Contrasting markedly with the uniformity of factory-workers' houses, the varied elevations of these cottages with their associated walks and workshops form a highly distinctive townscape. The abundance of this type of housing indicates that Bridport's industrial community did not immediately convert to the regulated way of life of the factory worker in the 19th century. Outworkers' cottages are often larger than contemporary factory-workers' housing, with a wider range of building materials, room layouts and architectural details. Many have rear extensions suitable for industrial use, such as a workshop or a turn house for the adjoining walk. Another common feature is a through-passage giving direct access from the street to the walk or workshop behind the cottage.

## Factory-workers' housing

Regular terraces of smaller houses, usually without provision for outworking, are widely associated with 19th-century industry in other areas, and are also found in Bridport and West Bay. They were often built within a more formal, planned development close to the workplace, which included new streets and community buildings. Perhaps the best-preserved early example in the Bridport area is in West Bay (Fig 36), where the regular layout of early 19th-century streets, terraced housing, manager's houses and well-spaced warehouses contrasts markedly with the more congested layout of other port towns. More examples can be seen close to North Mills, Priory Mills and Pymore, but the relatively small number of these terraces indicates that most of the factory workforce in Bridport must have continued to live in the earlier cottages near the town centre.

## Managers' and owners' houses

The smallest managers' houses in Bridport are two- or three-storeyed dwellings attached to a factory or warehouse. Good examples survive at Pymore, Priory Mills and close to most of the warehouses in West Bay. In the 18th century merchants or manufacturers often chose to live close to their main premises, such as a mill, warehouse or workshop, as was probably the case at Court House adjoining Gundry's Court Mills and at, the now demolished, Wykes Court on North Street. Up to the early 19th century merchants and manufacturers occupied some of the larger town houses, such as the South Street residence of Stephen Whetham of Priory Mills (Fig 37). Bridport's leading merchants and manufacturers were distinguished by the elegant Georgian or Victorian villas they built around the peripheries of the town. Downe Hall, for example, was built by William Downe, a prominent merchant whose nephew was one of the partners of Pymore Mills. The great success of the Gundry business saw the family move out of the town to a large Victorian country house, The Hyde, Walditch, overlooking Bridport from the east (Fig 38).

Figure 36 *(opposite, top) Swains Row, built close to Bridport Harbour in the 1820s, is a well-preserved example of formal industrial housing. [AA042465]*

Figure 37 *(opposite, bottom) This South Street townhouse was occupied by Stephen Whetham of Priory Mills from 1818. [DP000807]*

Figure 38 *(above) The Victorian country residence of the Gundry family, at Walditch. [DP004837]*

## The South-West Quadrant

Bridport's largest industrial suburb originated to the west of St Michael's Lane in the late 18th century and continued to expand up to the mid-20th century. It is bounded on the south by the Priory Mills complex and to the west by the course of the River Brit. In spite of extensive demolition and alteration, intact examples of all the building types of the local hemp and flax industry still survive in the area, including open and covered walks, warehousing, workshops, mills and housing. The South-West Quadrant is one of the earliest industrial suburbs in the country and is now the best illustration of the distinctive townscapes created by the expansion of Bridport from the late 18th century.

Development began on a greenfield site in the mid-18th century with the construction of a number of small cottages, some of which still survive, alongside the open meadow to the west of St Michael's Lane. Documentary evidence indicates that the land adjoining the cottages was sold off in lots from around 1800 and that most of the occupiers were connected with the hemp and flax industry. By the mid-19th century more industrial housing had been built, along with open and covered walks running westwards to the river and related industrial buildings such as turn houses, yarn stores and combing houses. Many of Bridport's most successful textile firms eventually occupied premises in the area. The construction or modification of buildings for the flax and hemp industry accelerated in the second half of the 19th century, including the addition of housing in some of the earlier open walks. By 1900 the character of the area had been completely transformed with its relatively new and densely-packed townscape of specialised buildings associated with the open and covered walks (Figs 39 and 40).

The best-preserved early buildings are grouped around the warehouse at No. 40 St Michael's Lane, along with its rear extensions, and the adjoining cottages to the north and south. Parts of these cottages date from the initial phase of building in the area. They include rear extensions or outbuildings which were related to the former open walks. A long alley to the rear of the warehouse is a former open walk, flanked on its north side by a two-storeyed, late 19th-century covered walk.

Figure 39 *The South-West Quadrant,* c*1950, when most of the covered walks were still intact. Some of the flat-roofed buildings still have their wartime camouflage paint. [Museum of Net Manufacture]*

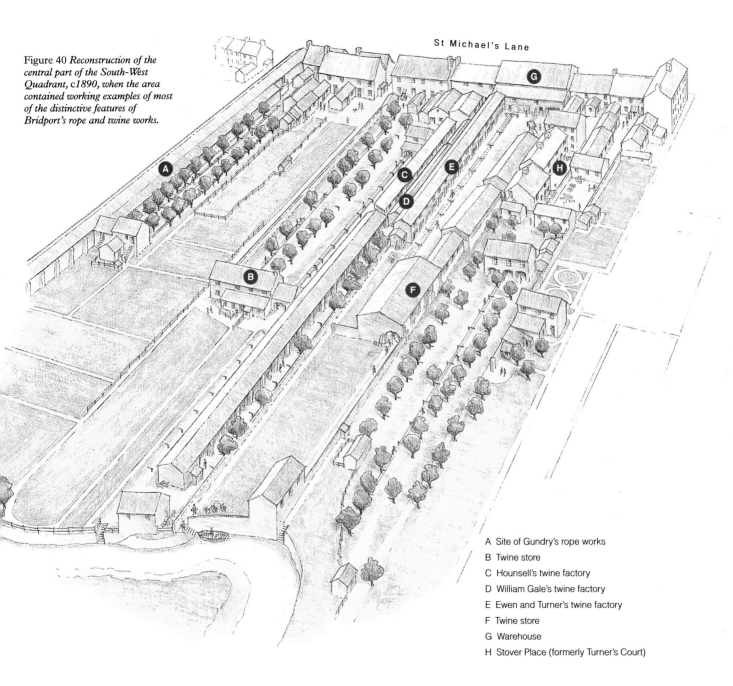

Figure 40 *Reconstruction of the central part of the South-West Quadrant, c1890, when the area contained working examples of most of the distinctive features of Bridport's rope and twine works.*

St Michael's Lane

A  Site of Gundry's rope works

B  Twine store

C  Hounsell's twine factory

D  William Gale's twine factory

E  Ewen and Turner's twine factory

F  Twine store

G  Warehouse

H  Stover Place (formerly Turner's Court)

Some of the windows have been blocked but in all other respects this is the best-preserved 19th-century walk building in Bridport (Fig 41).
To the south of the alley is a north-light shed built on the site of another former walk. Further west are two late 19th-century yarn stores and a very late example of a covered walk clad in corrugated-iron.

As the area later came under the control of larger firms, some of the 19th-century walks were replaced with wider north-light or flat-roofed sheds. Other later additions include buildings for the production of cordage and netting on machines and for the tarring and drying of twine or rope. The southern part of the area is dominated by the Bridport Industries building, a long two-storeyed factory in red brick with a prominent central clock tower (Fig 42). It was built in the early 20th century, retaining the plan form of an earlier rope works on the same site, and was the main building of the firm of William Edwards and Sons, who specialised in sports netting. Bridport Industries was formed in 1947

Figure 41 *The alley behind No. 40 St Michael's Lane was formerly an open walk. The two-storeyed late 19th-century building on the left is now the best-preserved covered walk in the central part of Bridport; similar buildings on the right were replaced by north-light sheds in the 1920s. [DP001484]*

Figure 42 *The Bridport Industries building, formerly of William Edwards and Sons, manufacturers of sports netting products. [DP005124]*

by the merger of Edwards and Sons with William Gale and Sons, the occupier of some of the walks to the north, and Hounsell's (Bridport) Limited of North Mills. In 1963 Bridport Industries was merged with Gundry's of Court Mills and Pymore to form Bridport-Gundry.

## West Bay: Bridport's harbour

Although Bridport is located about a mile inland from West Bay, the reconstruction of the harbour in the mid-18th century proved to be one of the most important events in the history of both the flax and hemp industry and the town itself. The availability of local shipping facilities, on a scale comparable to many larger port towns, gave Bridport a competitive advantage at a time before canals and railways benefited other industrial areas. The harbour was not built solely for the textile industry and was also used for a wide range of other commodities, but flax, hemp and textile products soon accounted for a significant proportion of its trade. By encouraging the development of international markets, in particular for netting and cordage, the harbour generated prosperity for the flax and hemp industry and so influenced the growth of Bridport's townscape. It also gave Bridport firms a strongly international outlook that has shaped the development of the industry up to the present day.

The first well-documented harbour was built in 1744 by the engineer John Reynolds, although it was probably not the earliest to be built on the River Brit. Boats had used the river to reach Bridport from at least the 13th century, and it is likely that some earlier form of harbour was sited close to the estuary and had become silted up. Reynolds' new harbour was roughly the same size and shape as that of today, with an L-shaped basin and two piers protecting the entrance from the sea. At the time it was built there was no direct road to Bridport and there were few buildings near the harbour except those grouped around the Bridport Arms. By the 1760s the shipyard had opened on a sloping site to the west of the harbour, and later expanded to become one of the most succesful

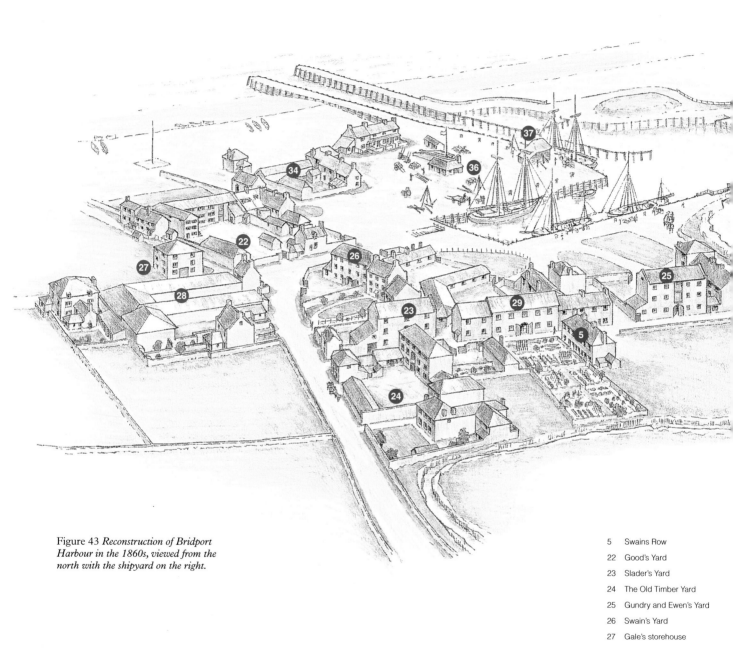

Figure 43 *Reconstruction of Bridport Harbour in the 1860s, viewed from the north with the shipyard on the right.*

| | |
|---|---|
| 5 | Swains Row |
| 22 | Good's Yard |
| 23 | Slader's Yard |
| 24 | The Old Timber Yard |
| 25 | Gundry and Ewen's Yard |
| 26 | Swain's Yard |
| 27 | Gale's storehouse |

shipyards in Dorset in the early 19th century. The mid-18th-century harbour needed frequent repairs and was gradually rebuilt over the next century, notably by John Rennie during the first decade of the 19th century, and by Francis Giles in 1824.

The main period of development around the harbour took place in the early to mid-19th century, when the addition of new streets, housing and warehouses created a largely self-contained community (Fig 43). Housing for workers, supervisors and merchants was required because of the relatively isolated position of the harbour. A new direct route from Bridport was built in 1819 (now called West Bay Road). At about the same time, George Street was laid out to the north of the harbour, along with three warehouses and two rows of terraced workers' houses on its south side. More warehouses were added shortly afterwards on George Street, West Bay Road and Station Road, along with another terrace of workers' housing on Swains Row (see Fig 36). William Swain was a local landowner and merchant who, for a time, occupied a large detached villa on the northern edge of the settlement, which is now the Haddon House Hotel. Other new buildings included a large lime kiln, which was probably used to provide mortar for building work close to the harbour, a crane house and a salt store, while the shipyard saw the addition of further housing and industrial structures, including a saw pit and a rope walk.

An indication of the significant but short-lived success of the harbour was its designation as a bond port between 1832 and 1881, which required both a local customs house and secure warehousing. In this period Bridport's maritime trade competed successfully with the older established harbours in neighbouring parts of Dorset and Devon, such as Poole, Weymouth and Exeter. In contrast with the congested nature of older port towns, however, the quays, streets, buildings and shipyard were newly-built and more efficiently arranged in a spacious layout. This was made possible by the separation of the town from its harbour and by the availability of level ground for building around the harbour site. The open layout also influenced the design of the warehouses, which at older ports were typically closely-packed between a pattern of narrow streets. At Bridport Harbour the warehouses were set well back from the quaysides and each comprised a group of related buildings. Most faced a secure walled yard which included a detached house for the owner or manager, a smaller counting house or office and usually additional storage sheds and awnings, although in many cases the various buildings adjoining the warehouses later passed into separate ownership.

After thriving for several decades, the fortunes of the harbour and shipyard began to change following the extension of the Great Western Railway to Bridport in 1857. The addition of a local branch line to the harbour in 1884 heralded a period of transition that saw the closure of the shipyard and the renaming of Bridport Harbour as West Bay in a bid to encourage tourism. The harbour was no longer a major asset to the flax and hemp industry, but trade in coal, hemp and other commodities continued on a smaller scale until the mid-20th century. The rise of tourism at West Bay was marked architecturally by the construction of the prominent Pier Terrace in 1885. Designed in the arts and crafts style by the architect E S Prior, this fashionable terrace of five large seaside residences was built on the site of the disused lime kiln (Fig 44).

## Good's Yard warehouse

The earliest warehouse in West Bay, and also the largest, was built to the east of the harbour in a position close to the beach. The site is named after its owners, the Good family, who occupied the nearby shipyard in the early 19th century and whose descendants occupied the warehouse throughout the 20th century. It may have been built in 1771, and was certainly extant by 1787. In this period Good's Yard and the Bridport Arms formed the centre of the settlement, before 19th-century expansion took place around George Street. In the early 19th century the warehouse was occupied by H B Way for the storage of flax, hemp, iron and wine. It is built to an L-shaped plan of three storeys and is the main building in a complex which includes a walled yard, several houses, a separate walled garden and various smaller 19th-century buildings (Fig 45). A second storehouse was formerly located on the west side of the yard. The warehouse itself has a number of early structural details, including stone-mullioned windows, external staircases and an unusual basement comprising a longitudinal barrel-vaulted ceiling with its apex supported

Figure 44 *Pier Terrace, built in 1885 on the site of the disused lime kiln, marks the transformation of Bridport's industrial harbour into the tourist resort of West Bay. [DP000712]*

Figure 45 *The late 18th-century Good's Yard is the oldest warehouse at West Bay, and the last to remain in industrial use. The early mullioned windows and external staircases contrast with the later features of the other nearby warehouses. [AA049610]*

by an arcaded spine wall (Fig 46). The basement is entered via a heavy studded door and may have been built to provide a secure storage area. The roof appears to have been replaced by the late 19th century, but the upper storeys retain many original features including wooden cranes, floor traps and wall panelling, and are now partly used as a net loft (Fig 47).

## 19th-century warehouses in West Bay

In the first half of the 19th century, seven more warehouses were added to the small community, mostly built along the newly laid-out streets, plus a separate salt store and other storage buildings in the shipyard. Warehouses are West Bay's dominant type of historic building and still provide a vivid reminder of the industrial and commercial origins of Bridport Harbour (Fig 48). They were used for a range of commodities,

Figure 46 *(above, left) The massively-built stone-vaulted basement of Good's Yard. [AA049582]*

Figure 47 *(above, right) A well-preserved timber crane in the wing of Good's Yard. [AA049599]*

Figure 48 *(opposite, top) All the buildings in this group at the south end of West Bay Road are converted 19th-century warehouses with associated housing. [AA049615]*

Figure 49 *(opposite, bottom) The Old Timber Yard warehouse on George Street, dating from the 1820s, showing the prominent taking-in doors found in the later warehouses. [AA049850]*

but flax and hemp were amongst the most common and their occupiers included some of the best-known Bridport manufacturers. The surviving buildings show a variety of structural and architectural details, indicating that they were built by different firms, but since they were intended to serve a similar purpose they also share a common range of functional features. Most had central loading bays for carts with overhead floor traps and a hand-powered hoist mechanism mounted between the roof trusses. External loading doors are positioned above the loading bay, and the later warehouses had a second set of doors for loading goods directly to and from the street (Fig 49). One consequence of the slow decline in the use of the West Bay warehouses in the 20th century is that their functional details are often well preserved, including several examples of internal wooden cranes and hoists.

CHAPTER 3

# A future for Bridport's industrial past

Bridport's flax and hemp industry is clearly of exceptional historic interest, and this ancient trade has rightfully become part of the town's identity and traditions. Comparison with historic industries in other regions gives us new insights into the broader significance of Bridport's industrial heritage, but also indicates that the more recent problems of Bridport's post-industrial areas are in many ways comparable with those of other towns and cities. Experience from elsewhere suggests that as Bridport continues to change, some of its most characteristic historic features could disappear if they are not appreciated and protected. In recognition of the need for positive action, to both regenerate and protect Bridport's distinctive historic areas, a range of initiatives have been undertaken in recent decades, including work by West Dorset District Council, Dorset County Council, English Heritage and the South West Regional Development Agency.

## The significance of Bridport's industrial heritage

To fully appreciate the significance of Bridport's industrial past the local heritage needs to be considered in a national context. Bridport's townscape stands out from other industrial towns because of its particular mix of distinctive buildings and landscapes, but also because the surviving industrial features cover such a wide range of dates. In other urban areas the mills, housing and infrastructure of the factory system generally replaced earlier building types, sometimes heralding a complete transformation of the landscape. In contrast, Bridport's factories were combined with a rebirth of the old industry and the development of the harbour, giving the town a notably wide variety of industrial buildings. Bridport firms also maintained unusually strong links with the surrounding countryside, originally through the use of locally-grown flax and hemp, resulting in the building of specialised mills and the use of outworkers over a wide area. Another indication of the relative success of the local textile industry, and its impact on the town, was the creation of the new industrial suburbs, such as the South-West Quadrant and the

*New sea defences and promenade, West Bay, taken in 2005. [DP000721]*

51

Figure 50 *Former twine store, warehouse and disused walks to the rear of Stover Place in the South-West Quadrant. [DP001482]*

Figure 51 *Mangerton Mill, located two miles north-east of Bridport, is a well-preserved example of a watermill used for both corn and locally-grown flax. [DP004834]*

Figure 52 *The wheel chamber of Mangerton Mill supplied power for both the mill stones and the flax-processing machinery, which were located in separate rooms on either side of the race. [DP005175]*

larger factory sites. These greenfield developments were a characteristic feature of Bridport, greatly increasing the size of the town. Contemporary examples in other regions were mostly built on the fringes of major cities.

The survival of so much of Bridport's industrial townscape into the 21st century is both rare and extremely fortunate. The removal of some old buildings has already changed the appearance of parts of the town, but the wholesale demolition of manufacturing industry, as seen in some other regions, has not occurred. This is partly due to crucial differences in the history of the local textile industry. In the 20th century Bridport's largest firms showed a resilience to the economic pressures which often led to the demise of traditional industries. The smaller firms were merged to form larger concerns which adapted to changing markets and then took over firms in other areas. The old trade saw a gradual decline lasting many decades, followed by the emergence of the more specialised industry of today. As a result industrial buildings remained in use for longer, including some of the distinctive factory buildings and walks, and are consequently relatively well-preserved. A similar process of adaptation leading to the survival of historic features had also occurred in the early 19th century, when factories were first introduced to Bridport. On that occasion the survival of small firms and the system of outworking led to the preservation of the open walks, cottages and other features of the pre-factory era.

## The future of Bridport's industrial heritage

In the early 21st century the need to do something about Bridport's historic industrial sites is becoming more urgent. The successful re-use of some industrial buildings, such as warehouses and mills, has already been demonstrated by enterprising property owners and developers. Other notable examples of the town's industrial architecture, however, have now been partially disused or derelict for a long time. Unfortunately, it is the parts of Bridport that benefited most from the great success of the flax and hemp industry that have seen the most change as the industry has

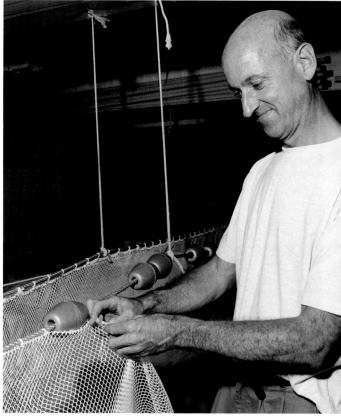

Figure 53 *(left) The manufacture of aircraft cargo restraint nets at Court Mills by AmSafe Bridport is now a multi-national business. [DP000858]*

Figure 54 *(right) Nets for fishing and other uses are manufactured by Collins Nets at Good's Yard, West Bay. [AA49601]*

contracted, and inevitably they include some historically-significant buildings. Making a successful future for such areas is often a matter of balancing a complex range of issues, but combining the best features of the past with economic regeneration can provide a viable future for places where none has been apparent for decades.

Figure 55 *An early 19th-century flax warehouse at Pymore, converted to flats with ground-floor garaging. [DP000798]*

Figure 56 *(above) The attic of the late 18th-century Good's Yard warehouse retains many historic features, including interior wooden cladding and roof structure. [AA049597]*

Figure 57 *(right) The attic of The Old Timber Yard warehouse, West Bay, transformed into an artist's studio with good preservation of the roof and hoist mechanism. [AA046235]*

Figure 58 *A recent domestic conversion, in traditonal materials, added to Slader's Yard warehouse, West Bay. [DP000804]*

Regeneration and conservation programmes aim to effectively manage economic and environmental problems which have developed over a long period. They do not often provide quick-fix solutions, but the benefits of heritage-oriented regeneration have already been demonstrated in industrial towns and cities in different parts of the country. For example on the South-West coast, towns such as Poole, Weymouth and Exeter have seen successful regeneration schemes centred on areas of maritime or industrial heritage, and similar initiatives have begun in Bridport. Regeneration programmes are developed through public consultation and depend for their success on partnerships between the private and public sectors. Local authorities take the lead role in bringing together property owners, developers, architects and the relevant regional and national agencies, with the aim of ensuring that development contributes positively to the best interests of the area. In Bridport, public consultation by West Dorset District Council in the 1990s showed a strong demand for the regeneration of former industrial sites, after which regeneration programmes have been initiated in two

Figure 59 *The recently-built sea defences and extension to the old Bridport Harbour, taken in 2005. [DP000735]*

Figure 60 *Apartments under construction at West Bay reflect the architectural details of the harbour's historic warehouses, also taken in 2005. [DP000722]*

areas of great importance to the historic flax and hemp industry, the South-West Quadrant and West Bay.

To assist the combined aims of regeneration and conservation two complementary forms of heritage protection are available, the listing of buildings of historic or architectural interest and the designation of Conservation Areas. In Bridport these are carried out respectively by English Heritage and West Dorset District Council. Listing aims to protect the best examples of each building type in a national context, taking into account the survival of architecturally and historically-significant details. The designation of a Conservation Area offers a more general level of protection, recognising the contribution of a wide range of buildings and other features to the character of a place, including buildings of local historic interest which are not listed. Notable examples in Bridport include the walls, workshops and other small structures associated with the former open walks. Bridport's Conservation Area was extended in 2000 to include more of the South-West Quadrant in recognition of its significance. More recently, Conservation Area appraisals have been

Figure 61 *Tannery Yard, Bridport, showing an effective reuse of industrial buildings and the retention of traditional building materials in a Conservation Area. [AA045615]*

Figure 62 *Part of the Bridport Conservation Area in South Street, an area of former outworkers' cottages, many of which are now protected as listed buildings. [DP000751]*

completed for both Bridport and West Bay, following extensive consultation, which identify the locally-significant buildings and specify the range of features characterised by the flax and hemp industry.

In the early 21st century Bridport may have reached a turning point. For centuries the skills and enterprise of local people have generated an unrivalled tradition of manufacturing industry, a tradition which pre-dates England's Industrial Revolution and yet has survived longer than many industries in other areas. The manufacture of twine, rope, nets and sailcloth has also left another legacy, however, one with an uncertain future for run-down historic buildings and derelict sites. All towns evolve, but their historic environment gives an immediate impression of the character, achievements and sense of pride of the community that built them; the buildings described in this book show how Bridport's industry has changed over the centuries, and how extensively it has shaped the townscape. Further change in Bridport is inevitable, but the benefits and the demand for sustainable regeneration have been demonstrated. As the significance of its townscapes and buildings is being revealed, Bridport has a rare opportunity to protect its unique heritage and to promote its special place in industrial history.

Figure 63 *St Michael's Lane, the historic entrance to Bridport's largest industrial suburb. [AA049074]*

# Glossary

**Balling mill** A small, specialised mill containing water-powered machinery for stamping or softening hemp. The process followed the initial breaking-up of the woody stems by *swingling*.

**Beam** In commercial fishing, a strong wooden or metal attachment used to support the open mouth of a trawl net. Bridport firms supplied beams and other fittings, in addition to the nets themselves.

**Braiding** The production of netting and shaped-net products, traditionally by hand, from knotted twine.

**Burgage plots** A common form of land ownership in medieval towns, comprising long, narrow, parallel plots extending at right angles from the main streets. Often fronted by a house and used for cultivation or industry, the far ends of the plots were sometimes linked by a back lane.

**Burh** A defended place, part of a defensive system set up across southern Britain by King Alfred during the late 9th century. Some Anglo-Saxon burhs were planned as towns with a regular grid pattern of streets and properties within the defences.

**Combing** In the Bridport flax and hemp industry, an alternative term for *heckling* (used for other processes in the worsted and cotton industries).

**Covered walk** A distinctive long, narrow building used for the production of twine or rope. Usually one or two storeys, with pitched or gabled roofs and small windows or opening ventilation panels. Can take the form of an open-sided awning. Sometimes built on the site of former *open walks*.

**Dew retting** The initial breaking-down of cut hemp or flax by leaving it to partially rot in the fields (*see retting*).

**Heckling** The separation and cleaning of the longest fibres from a bundle of cut flax or hemp by manually dragging it through a row of fixed metal spikes. Sometimes carried out by powered machinery (*see also tow*).

**Integration** In historic textile mills, vertical integration refers to the combination of the full range of processes from raw material to finished product at one site, often requiring distinctive buildings for each stage of production. Horizontal integration refers to the organisation of successive stages at different sites owned by the same firm.

**Jack** A small machine fixed at the end of a walk, comprising a set of rotating hooks turned by a hand crank or by power. Prepared yarns were tied to the hooks and twisted into twine, or lengths of twine laid to make rope.

**Jumper loom** A type of large powered loom for making some types of netting, introduced extensively in Bridport mills by the late 19th century. The mechanism was activated by the operative standing on a treadle.

**Loomshop** A distinctive type of building in which hand looms were concentrated so that cloth production could be organised under one roof. Pre-dating the introduction of powered factories, they were built in many of the early textile areas, usually reflecting the local style of vernacular architecture.

**North-light shed** A type of single-storeyed factory building associated with 19th-century textile mills, often covering a large area with many distinctive asymmetrical roof ridges. Glazing was located on the steeper sides of the ridges, which were often built to face north to give even internal lighting.

**Open walk** A long, rectangular piece of open land used for the production of yarn, twine or rope, often associated with small industrial buildings and defined by boundary walls. Some of Bridport's *burgage plots* were used as early walks. Later, open walks were built alongside the *covered walks*.

**Outworking** The production of cloth and netting in home-based workshops, using materials supplied by a merchant. The practice survived in Bridport far longer than in other industrial areas.

**Putting-out system** The system of production that was widespread before factories. Raw materials were distributed by a merchant, often from a warehouse, to skilled workers who made the finished product at home or in a workshop (*see outworking*).

**Proto-industry** The term used in economic history to describe the long transitional period leading up to the introduction of the factory system in the late 18th century.

**Retting** The initial breaking-down of cut flax or hemp, either by soaking in water in a retting tank or by *dew retting*.

**Size, Sizing** A protective coating, comprising a starch-like mixture, which was applied to yarn, twine or cloth, enabling it to resist abrasion and prevent rot.

**Skirder** A horizontal bracket supported by a post used to support the lengths of yarn, twine or rope along an *open* or *covered walk*. Pegs or wires on top of the bracket were used to separate the yarn.

**Stook, stooking** The traditional method of drying cut flax in the field by forming it into a series of upright cones.

**Swingling** The breaking up of cut flax and hemp to separate the useful fibre from the hard woody stems. Water-powered swingling machinery was first used in the Bridport area in 1803, at Burton Bradstock.

**Tar, tarring** Liquid tar was commonly applied as a finish to yarns, ropes and cables intended for use at sea to prevent rot.

**Turn house** A small one- or two-storeyed building facing the end of an *open walk*. The ground floor was open, protecting the *jack* and its operative. The upper floor was sometimes used as a workshop or twine store.

**Tow** The short lengths of waste fibre obtained as a by-product of *heckling*, used to make lower-grade yarns.

# Further reading

Baines, P 1985 *Flax and Linen*. Princes Risborough: Shire (Shire Album 133)

Bone, M 1985 'The Bridport Flax and Hemp Industry'. *Bristol Ind Archaeol Soc J*, **18**, 19–31

Crick, M M, 1908 'The Hemp Industry'. *Victoria History of the County of Dorset*, vol 2, 344–53. London: Constable

Gosling, G, 1999 *Bridport Past*. Chichester: Phillimore

Keystone Historic Building Consultants, 2000 'West Bay, Dorset, Historical Report'. Unpublished report for West Dorset District Council

Legg, R, 2003 *The Book of Bridport: Town, Harbour and West Bay*. Tiverton: Halsgrove

Martin, C, 2003 *The Bridport Trade, Rope and Net: Hemp and Flax*. Bridport: Constanduros Press

Over, L 1988 *Bridport: The Evolution of a Town*. Bridport: Bridport Museum Publication No.1

Pahl, J 1960 'The Rope and Net Industry of Bridport: Some Aspects of its History and Geography'. *Dorset Natur Hist Archaeol Soc/Proc* **82**, 143–54

Perry, P J 1964 'Bridport Harbour and the Hemp and Flax Trade, 1815–1914'. *Dorset Natur Hist Archaeol Soc/Proc* **86**, 231–4

Sanctuary, A 1980 *Rope, Twine and Net Making*. Princes Risborough: Shire (Shire Album 15)

The Garden History Society and the Dorset Gardens Trust, 2001 'The Landscape and Gardens of South-West Bridport'. Unpublished report for West Dorset District Council

Trenchard, D 2000 *Dorset People Involved in the Growing of Hemp and Flax 1782–1793*. Bridport: the Somerset & Dorset Family History Society

# Other titles in this series

*The Birmingham Jewellery Quarter: An introduction and guide.* John Cattell and Bob Hawkins, 2000. Product code 50204, ISBN 1850747776

*'One Great Workshop': The buildings of the Sheffield metal trades.* Nicola Wray, Bob Hawkins and Colum Giles, 2001. Product code 50214, ISBN 1873592663

*Manchester: The Warehouse Legacy – An introduction and guide.* Simon Taylor, Malcolm Cooper and P S Barnwell, 2002. Product code 50668, ISBN 1873592671

*Newcastle's Grainger Town: An urban renaissance.* Fiona Cullen and David Lovie, 2003. Product code 50811, ISBN 1873592779

*Gateshead: Architecture in a changing English urban landscape.* Simon Taylor and David Lovie, 2004. Product code 52000, ISBN 1873592760

*Storehouses of Empire: Liverpool's historic warehouses.* Colum Giles and Bob Hawkins, 2004. Product code 50920, ISBN 1873592809

*Built to Last? The buildings of the Northamptonshire boot and shoe industry.* Kathryn A Morrison with Ann Bond, 2004. Product code 50921, ISBN 1873592795

*Behind the Veneer: The South Shoreditch Furniture Trade and its Buildings.* Joanna Smith and Ray Rogers, 2006. Product code 51204, ISBN-10 1873592965, ISBN-13 9781873592960

£7.99 each (plus postage and packing)

To order, tel: EH Sales 01761 452966
Email: ehsales@gillards.com

Online bookshop: www.english-heritage-books.org.uk

Back cover
*Net making at Uploders, near Bridport, 1930s.*
*[Crown Copyright Reserved]*

## Map of Bridport and West Bay showing town-centre streets *c*1900

### KEY

#### Housing

1 South Street cottages
2 East Street cottages
3 North Allington cottages
4 St Michael's Lane cottages
5 Swains Row and George Street housing, West Bay
6 The residence of Stephen Whetham, South Street
7 Court House, residence of Joseph Gundry
8 Downe Hall, residence of William Downe

#### Walks

9 Open walks, East Street
10 Open walks, North Allington
11 Open walks, South Street
12 Open and covered walks, St Michael's Lane
13 Covered walks, West Allington
14 Covered walk, North Mills

#### Workshops

15 2 St Michael's Lane
16 Folly Mill Lane
17 Foundry Lane
18 Rax Lane

#### Warehouses

19 Stephen Whetham's warehouse, Gundry Lane
20 Warehouse, St Michael's Lane
21 North Mills warehouse
22 Good's Yard, West Bay
23 Slader's Yard, West Bay
24 The Old Timber Yard, West Bay
25 Gundry and Ewen's Yard, West Bay
26 Swain's Yard, West Bay
27 Gale's Storehouse, West Bay
28 Site of Cox and Goode's Warehouse, West Bay
29 Site of Selwood and Whetham's Yard, West Bay
30 Salt Store, West Bay

#### Other sites

31 Former drying ground and walk, Court Mills
32 Bridport Industries building
33 Twine stores
34 The Bridport Arms, West Bay
35 Site of former Railway Station, West Bay
36 Pier Terrace, West Bay (site of former lime kiln)
37 Site of former crane house, West Bay